Westcountry Outlaws Highwaymen & Rogues

Published by:
Shark Cornwall Publishing, 20 Dean Clarke House,
Southernhay, Exeter, EX1 1AP.
First published 2023

ISBN no. 978-0-9558694-8-8
Photographs: Richard Peirce
Layout and Design: Michelle Panter
Printed by Booths Print, The Praze, Penryn, Cornwall, TR10 8AA

BY THE SAME AUTHOR
Pirates of Devon & Cornwall
Execution Sites in Devon & Cornwall
West Country Witches, Wizards & Warlocks
Sharks in British Seas
Giant Steps
Sharks of Cornwall & Devon
U.K. Great White Shark Enigma
Shark Attack Britain
The Poachers Moon
Nicole
Cuddle Me, Kill Me
Orca
Pangolins, Scales of Injustice
Kalahari Gold
66 True Kalahari Stories

Dedication

This book is dedicated to all victims of crime everywhere. Yesterday's pirates, outlaws, highwaymen and footpads, are today's internet scammers and identity fraudsters. I hope they all get caught!

Richard

Thanks & Acknowledgements

R.D. Blackmore (Lorna Doone)

Neil Britton

Sqeez D'Souza

Sarah Doggart

Google

Helpful Holidays (Highwayman Hauntings of Devon)

Matt Devenish

Gerald Norris (Westcountry Rogues & Outlaws)

Steve & Frances Lee

Mike Long

Michelle Panter

Jacqui Peirce

Perry Richardson

Shutterstock

Angela Tate

Westcountry Outlaws Highwaymen and Rogues

I guess I am as much a sucker for the Hollywood image of our villains as many others. When I see the police in films chasing a highwayman, unless he is a really bad guy, I usually hope he gets away. Nevertheless, this is a history book, and although I have tried to make it a fun read, it must be factual and as accurate as possible, so I have had to resist the temptation to turn villains into heroes, and have stuck to the facts. When researching and taking photographs for this book I often drove across the moors of Devon and Cornwall, and in many places, even today, it doesn't take much imagination to envisage footpads, thieves, and highwaymen lying in wait for the unwary.

This is the fourth in what I call my 'black book series', and researching and writing these books has been great fun and hugely rewarding in many ways. It has added new dimensions to familiar places, and greatly enriched the experience of travelling around the Westcountry. I hope that for both residents and visitors alike I manage to sprinkle a little magic dust in various places, give them a new dimension, and bring them alive in a different way.

Our outlaws, highwaymen and rogues were a colourful bunch, I hope you enjoy meeting them.

Richard Peirce

Westcountry Outlaws, Highwaymen & Rogues

Introduction

The term 'highway robbery' originates from acts of theft on highways and byways. From around the 1600's to the early 1900's footpads and thieves on horseback attacked travellers on Britain's roads. The roads which crossed the Westcountry's lonely moors were excellent places for these rogues and villains to lie in wait for unsuspecting travellers. Robbers mounted on horseback were generally known as highwaymen, whereas the thieves on foot carried a less romantic label and were called footpads. Whether mounted or on foot the usual method of attack was from ambush. Thieves would lie in wait in hedges, or behind bushes or rocks before leaping out to surprise their hapless victims. Knives, clubs, firearms, and larger blades like cutlasses and swords were all used to threaten travellers, and force them to part with their valuables.

Dartmoor, Exmoor, Bodmin Moor and lonely stretches of road in other remote locations were ideal places for these criminals to operate in. These areas were mostly sparsely populated, and there was very limited police presence so the chances of getting caught were minimal. As well as those travelling between towns and cities on horseback, in coaches, or on foot, farmers returning from market were frequently targeted. The poor farmer would be returning home from market having sold livestock or produce only to be robbed and, often badly beaten up. It was quite common for farmers to band together and be armed to guard against attack. Penalties for getting caught for highway robbery might be considered harsh today. If victims were seriously injured or even killed, then the culprit, if caught, risked death by hanging. In less serious cases the criminal would often be transported to the colonies.

There were enormous differences in the type of villains involved in robbery on the highways. At one end of the spectrum were the footpads who were often half starving petty thieves, many of whom had been in wars in the army or navy before being discharged. These people were used to violence and adept in the use of weapons. Because their escape was on foot their attack would often be very violent, not only to enable robbery, but also to prevent or deter pursuit, whereas thieves on horseback could get away much more quickly. At the other end of the spectrum were the mounted highwaymen like Dick Turpin and Tom Faggus. Although, like the footpads, they were just actually highway robbers, folklore often grew up around these highwaymen, and Tom Faggus was considered, and considered himself, to be something of a Robin Hood type character.

As the decades passed various factors made highway robbery more difficult, and chances of getting caught improved. Motor vehicles were much more difficult to stop than riders, horse drawn carriages, or pedestrians. Cheques were introduced which reduced the amount of cash being carried by travellers. Better communications, more effective policing, increased use of roads and greater mobility all played their part in consigning the old-style highway robbers to history.

Today although thankfully not too common, we have muggers and car hijacking, and as well as money, jewellery, watches and other valuables, credit cards, cell phones, laptop computers and other present day articles have all been added to what thieves steal.

CHAPTER ONE

John Barnes

While he was the innkeeper at the Black Horse in South Street in Exeter John Barnes was an enthusiastic and apparently committed strict Presbyterian. His hostelry was often used for meetings by those who shared his faith and beliefs. The inn no longer exists, but used to stand near the old South Gate and the Holy Trinity Church, not one of these buildings still stands today.

Barnes was the Black Horse landlord in the 1670's probably between 1670 and 1677. He kept a clean, well-run tavern and was respected in his community. His wife Mary also had a good reputation, and was regarded as being virtuous, pious, quiet, tidy and respectable. The couple had nine children three of which were born during their time at the Black Horse.

It appears that something profound must have happened in 1676/77, because the family left the Black Horse and moved to an inn in Cullompton to the northeast of Exeter. The move to Cullompton signalled a complete change in Barnes' character, and the once well-respected zealous Presbyterian abandoned his previous lifestyle and became lazy, extravagant, unreliable, dissolute, and a liar. Within a short time he had got into debt and one of his main creditors was a blacksmith. Barnes couldn't or wouldn't repay the blacksmith, and in mid-1678 the blacksmith's pleas for the return of his money became more and more insistent. Barnes must have been a persuasive character, because not only had he convinced the blacksmith to part with his money, but when the pressure really came on, he persuaded the blacksmith to join him in a robbery to solve both of their financial problems.

The Exeter Carrier was a coach which journeyed from Exeter to London, it was known to carry large sums of money, and due to this the coach always travelled with trained armed guards. Barnes proposed to the blacksmith that they stop the coach and rob it on its way out of Honiton which was a major staging post at that time. The blacksmith agreed to join the venture, and Barnes also recruited a wool comber to his little gang. In those days Devon was a major producer of wool, and wool combers were employed to comb out and disentangle the fibres.

Barnes' plan was to waylay the coach at the top of the long hill which goes from outside Honiton on the road to Chard. The area he chose was almost uninhabited which was seen as a great advantage, and he believed that because Honiton was a good distance from their hometown of Cullompton, none of them would be recognised. Today it seems strange that a distance of only twelve miles was regarded as being far enough from home to make the chance of being recognised unlikely. Through contacts from his days in Exeter Barnes was able to find out on what date the next large shipment of money would be made and at what time.

The coach probably left Honiton in the darkness of early morning as it made its way on the next stage of its journey to London. When the team of four horses were at the beginning of the long hill the guards would have got down from the coach and walked beside it to the top. Barnes and his two accomplices lay in wait in ambush at the top of the hill, and would have heard the tinkle of horse bells and the drivers talking as the coach got nearer. Barnes and the others are said to have "leaped from behind some thorn bushes upon the carriers, and presented loaded pistols to their heads". The guards offered no resistance and the highwaymen took the money and other valuables, loaded their horses and made their getaway.

Barnes' plan to avoid being recognised was sensible but he hadn't fully thought it through. There may have been only a tiny chance that anyone from Cullompton would be on the coach, but the guards were from Exeter where Barnes had been well known. More than one of the guards recognised him, but because they were being held at gunpoint and in fear of their lives, they gave no sign of recognition. However, as soon as they could they reported Barnes, and he and the other two novice highwaymen from Cullompton were soon arrested and put in Exeter prison. Before being taken to prison the blacksmith had managed to hide a file in his clothing, and during their first night in jail they used the file to get out of their chains and escape. The blacksmith got clean away, but Barnes and the wool comber were soon recaptured.

They were both sentenced to hang on the 13th August 1678, and despite many pleas for clemency from women who knew Barnes' wife, and wanted to help the family by having him spared, he was executed. The execution almost certainly occurred at the Heavitree Drop, which was also known as Ringswell, and was situated at Gallows Cross where the road to Heavitree splits for Sidmouth.

The Barnes' gang had stolen £600.00 from the Exeter Carrier which was a huge fortune in those days, and which would have kept all three men and their families for the rest of their lives. Although he was a novice highwaymen John Barnes' only criminal job had resulted in a very large haul, and if bad luck and a hole in his planning had not resulted in him being recognised, he might well have got away with it.

Gallows Cross where the road to Heavitree splits for Sidmouth

Gallows Cross in 2022

CHAPTER TWO

Mary Bryant

Mary Bryant is a name to conjure with. Her occupation is listed as "Thief and Highwaywoman". She was born Mary Broad to William Broad and Dorothy Guillett in Lanlivery in Cornwall in 1765, and was baptised in Fowey on May 1st that year. Some accounts describe her father (William Broad) as a farmer, while others refer to him as a fisherman and mariner. The family was said to be "eminent for sheep stealing"!

In 1786 Mary and two accomplices, Catherine Fryer and Mary Hayden were convicted of highway robbery having assaulted and robbed Agnes Lakeman on a road in Plymouth. They stole a silk bonnet valued at 12 pence, and other goods, jewellery, and cash worth £1.00 and 11 shillings. All three of the accused were sentenced to hang. However, the judge commuted this sentence to seven years transportation.

She was first held on the hulk *Dunkirk* off Plymouth, and then transhipped to the *Charlotte* bound for Botany Bay in Australia. On the way to Australia Mary gave birth to a baby girl in Cape Town, the father of which was William Bryant who had been a Cornish fisherman, who had also been sentenced to be transported, and who she married after reaching Australia. William Bryant's offence had been that of having impersonated another seaman in order to receive his wages. In 1790 Mary's second child, a boy called Emanuel was born. The penal colony was at Port Jackson, and William's skill as a fisherman got him the job of being in charge of fishing to help feed the colony. However, in February 1789 he was convited of selling some of his catch privately and was sentenced to 100 lashes.

Mary Bryant

In October 1790 the Dutch vessel *Waaksamheyd* under Captain Detmier Smit arrived in Port Jackson badly in need of provisions and supplies. Bryant became friendly with Smit and was suspected of planning to escape and so was closely watched. Nevertheless in March 1791 William, Mary, their children and some other convicts all made their escape.

Their voyage was a 5237 km epic which ended 69 days later in June when they reached Koepang (Kupang) in Timor, Indonesia. The party posed as shipwreck victims, but the truth came out and they were arrested and detained. In October that year Captain Edward Edwards took the prisoners on board the *Rembang* and they reached Batavia, in what is today Jakarta Indonesia, in November. William and Emanual died on the island, and Mary, her daughter Charlottle, and other convicts were all shipped back to England. Charlotte died on the voyage so only Mary reached England where she was eventually pardoned.

Mary returned to her native Cornwall and rejoined her family. The last that is known of her was in November 1794 when she acknowledged receipt of a gift from James Boswell who had been a leading campaigner in obtaining her release and pardon. Boswell had campaigned for Mary when she returned to England and had continued to support her after her return to Cornwall.

Many words today are over used or used inappropriately, and one such word is epic. However, to use the word epic to describe the story and life of Mary Bryant is wholly fitting. This young Cornish woman was among the first to be transported to Australia, and was then one of the first to make a successful escape. She had a family in captivity and they all perished, but she survived and ended her life in Cornwall where it had begun. Her escape voyage in an open boat with her family and other convicts was an extraordinary feat of courage and determination. The others on board needed only to be concerned for their own survival, but Mary was a mother who would have been more concerned for her children than for herself. Her story has inspired books and a 2005 film called "The Incredible Journey of Mary Bryant", starring Romola Garai and Jack Davenport.

The Saints Way, Cornwall – Lanlivery to Fowey

CHAPTER THREE

Cruel Coppinger

Cruel Coppinger is a name to conjure with and has a leading place in Cornish folklore.

It is perhaps inevitable that with such a name it is difficult to separate fact and legend. A Coppinger undoubtedly did exist, although some believe there were two men called Coppinger either of which might have been the basis for the Coppinger of legend. I think the best way of telling the story of Cruel Coppinger is to do it in two parts, and start with the legend then move on to what is supposed to be fact.

The Legend of Cruel Coppinger

Legend has it that in the 1790's one night in a massive storm a ship got into trouble off Marsland Mouth in North Cornwall. The ship was visible from the shore and, as was common, a crowd of locals gathered on the beach to await any spoils that might be washed ashore from the wreck. The locals watched as the lone figure of a large man stood on the deck before leaping into the sea and swimming and wading to shore through the turbulent surf.

When the man reached the beach he grabbed the cloak off an old woman, wrapped himself in it, and jumped onto a horse on which a young woman was already mounted. He made off with the young woman and her horse, and went to her house where he installed himself as an uninvited permanent guest. The man said his name was Coppinger and that he came from Denmark. The girl was said to be called Dinah Hamlyn and eventually she married Coppinger. Somehow Coppinger the shipwrecked Dane made enough money to buy himself a house and some land, and he became the leader of a Cornish gang of smugglers, pirates, and wreckers known as the "Cruel Gang". To deter unwanted attention from the police and from revenue officers, the gang would often kill those law enforcement officials who were unlucky enough to get in their way. One part of the legend has it that a member of the Cruel Gang once beheaded a revenue officer.

The Cruel Gang carried out all sorts of illegal operations including piracy. He is reputed to have used several ships one of which was the *Black Prince* which attacked vessels on the Devon and Cornwall coasts, and in the English Channel. Coppinger's treatment of his family would have helped earn him the nickname 'Cruel'. It is said that when his father-in-law died he threatened to beat his wife with a horrific whip called a cat-o-nine-tails, unless his mother-in-law gave him all the money she had been left by her deceased husband.

His son was born a deaf mute who would patrol the cliff tops laughing, and legend has it that when he once saw the dead body of a local child lying on the beach below the cliffs, he laughed and giggled with glee as he pointed at the body. It is suspected that he might have thrown the child off the cliff. That he was born a deaf mute, and was thought not to have a soul was believed by locals to be due to his father's sins.

Eventually to avoid capture by the revenue men Coppinger comandeered a small boat and made his way out to a ship anchored off shore. It was a rough night and as soon as he was aboard the ship set sail and disappeared into the storm. The man who had terrorised North Cornwall sailed away never to be seen again.

In 1866 the Reverend Robert Stephen Hawker of Morwenstowe published a collection of Cornish legends among which was the tale of Cruel Coppinger. Four years later in his book *Footprints of Famous Men in North Cornwall* Hawker again refers to Coppinger. It is certain that Hawker's writings were the basis for much of the legend.

History and Potential Fact

Two real Coppingers, and maybe a combination of both of them, are likely to have inspired the legend of the Danish rogue. John Coppinger was of Danish descent and he arrived in Cornwall around 1793. He was probably from Ireland and may have left Cork in 1760 and moved to Brittany. Then in 1793 during the French Revoloution he moved to an estate near St. Austell in South Cornwall, which he may have used as a base for smuggling contraband from Brittany to Cornwall. John Coppinger's smuggling activities in South Cornwall do tie up with some of the exploits attributed to Cruel Coppinger and his gang in the English Channel.

Daniel Coppinger however is in many ways much closer to the man in the legend. He was shipwrecked in 1792 and married a girl called Hamlyn, although her name was Elizabeth or Ann rather than Dinah as in the legend. He lived near Hartland which puts him in the same area as his legendary namesake and was known to be a pirate and a smuggler.

One of the window panes at Galsham Farm near Hartland had his signature scratched on it and it survived intact until 1916. Thus different aspects of both Coppingers appear in the legend but it seems to be more based on Daniel than John Coppinger.

Sea caves at Marsland Mouth in North Cornwall

CHAPTER FOUR

The Doones

R.D. Blackmore's story of *Lorna Doone* is well known. Not so well known are the stories of the actual real life Doones.

Lorna Doone was first published in 1869. Before then in 1853 a book called *"A Guide Containing a Short Historical Sketch of Lifton, Lynmouth, Ilfracombe, and Places Adjacent in North Cornwall*, written by Thomas Henry Cooper, was published in North Devon. In this guide the Doones of Bagworthy are referred to as a successful band of robbers who had taken up residence in a small settlement of eleven cottages near Bagworthy Wood in what was then a remote part of Exmoor. The Doones were said not to be natives of Devon or Somerset, but to have been displaced by the Civil War, and during the period of Cromwell's Commonwealth they moved to Exmoor.

One night the Doones are reputed to have attacked a farmhouse called Yenworthy on the left of the Lynton and Porlock Road. They were shot at from an upstairs window by a woman firing a long duck or goose gun. The Doones abandonded their attack and retreated in the direction of Bagworthy leaving a significant blood trail for many miles. One evening before dark they broke into a house near Exford where they murdered a baby. The murder was said to have been witnessed by a woman servant who hid in the oven.

The murder triggered a huge response, and a large force of locals went to the Doones' hideout and took them into custody.

In 1854 another book was published which mentioned the Doones, and described them as a gang of bloodthirsty robbers who haunted the roads of Exmoor and ravaged the area in the reign of Charles I. One belief was that the Doones were a high ranking family which had left their homes at the end of the Civil War. In 1857 two more publications appeared which mentioned the family. *The North Devon Handbook* and an article *Wanderings on Exmoor*, the latter goes into more detail about the murder of the baby, and alleges that the Doones cooked and ate the child!

Next came *The Doones of Exmoor* which was a 22,000 word short book which was published in instalments in the magazine *The Leisure Hour*. It is generally accepted that *The Doones of Exmoor* provided the inspiration for R.D. Blackmore's classic *Lorna Doone*. Blackmoore began writing in early 1867 and finished the book in April the following year. He offered it to magazines to serialise and to book publishers, and got very little interest from either. Eventually a small print run of 500 copies went ahead and they sold very slowly. Then on the 10th October 1870 an unforseen event occurred which transformed the book into a sensation and a bestseller. An engagement was announced between the Queen's fourth daughter, Princess Louise, and the son of the Duke of Argyll, the Marquess of Lorne. This was seen as a true love match and it captured public imagination. As soon as the public realised that the Lorna Doone in the book was a relation of the real life Lornes the book took off. The publishers, Samson Low, reacted quickly to this huge unexpected publicity boost, and printed a lot more copies which were sold at the reduced price of six shillings which made it affordable to a wider public. Sales of the book never wavered and in 1897, three years before Blackmore's death, 100,000 copies of a new sixpenny edition sold out within a week.

North Devon and Exmoor signpost for walkers

The whole story of the Doones is clouded by claim and counter claim, theory and counter theory. Where they actually came from, why they retreated to a remote part of Exmoor, and what their real origins were are puzzles which will never be able to be answered by finding hard fact. What is certain is that the Doones of Exmoor did exist, and were a violent family of criminals who terrorised their local area. Maybe one of the enduring strengths of the Doones, and the reason for the fascination in which they are still held by many, is that mystery will always surround the real Doones, as opposed to Blackmore's fictional characters.

The area around Bagworthy is famed as having been the home of the legendary Doones

CHAPTER FIVE

Tom Faggus

Tom Faggus is the Westcountry's best known highwayman and legend has it that he was something of a Robin Hood. He never stole from the rich, often gave to the poor, and avoided violence. It is appropriate that the chapter on Faggus should follow the Doones because Blackmore features Faggus in his novel. The Faggus in *Lorna Doone* marries his cousin Annie, who is the sister of John Ridd, a lead character in the story. The fictional Faggus obtains a royal pardon for his highwayman activities and becomes a prosperous farmer. The likely story behind the real Faggus, who inspired Blackmore's character, is rather different, and it is what is known of the earlier actual Faggus that I will concentrate on.

Tom Faggus is most often referred to as coming from North Molton in Devon. In the early stage of his working life he was a blacksmnith, and his forge was next to an old pub called the Poltimore Arms. He was a successful blacksmith who won prizes for his work at local agricultural shows. Unfortunately he got into a legal quarrel with a powerful local family called Bampfylde who lived at Court Hall. Faggus lost the legal battle, was ruined financially, and he also lost the girl he was intending to marry. He was engaged to Betsy Paramore of South Molton, but when her father learned of the change in Faggus's circumstances he cancelled the wedding.

Misfortune had changed Faggus's life dramatically in every way, and he became a highwayman to make his living. In some respects Tom Faggus is only half of his own story, the other half is his remarkable strawberry roan mare which was called Winnie. Winnie's exploits convinced many that she possessed magical powers.

The 'gentleman' highway robber was soon a legend in his own time on Exmoor and the surrounding area, and attempts to catch him were numerous. A tip off alerted locals on one occasion near Exford and they formed a vigilante band lying in ambush for Faggus near Exford Bridge. Faggus was travelling in disguise when he appeared out of the mist and those waiting in ambush did not recognise him. The highwayman rode into the group and asked what they were waiting for? He was told they were waiting to arrest the robber Tom Faggus. Faggus immediately said that he was also looking for the highwayman as he had a score to settle with him. He joined the party so was actually waiting in ambush for himself!! After a while he suggested that in order to be properly prepared for the villain when he arrived, they should discharge their firearms and re-load them in case the powder had got damp in the wet misty weather. The ambush party all fired their guns into the air, all except Faggus. When he was sure he was the only one with loaded pistols, he told them who he was, collected all their money and valuables and galloped off. This was only one of many times when he avoided being captured. On another occasion a house in which he was hiding in Porlock was surrounded by armed locals, and they were confident they had him trapped . Somehow Faggus contrived to poke his hat out of the chimney, and those surrounding the buildings shot at it thinking he was trying to escape over the roof. While they were reloading the front door of the house burst open and, mounted on Winnie, Faggus appeared and galloped off unscathed by the hail of bullets which followed him.

Later when Faggus was being held at gunpoint near Dulverton, Winnie intervened by rearing up and knocking the pistol out of the hand of Faggus's captor. He had another close shave when the landlord of the Exmoor Arms in Simonsbath realised that the customer passing time drinking ale in his pub was none other than the notorious highwayman, and he sent someone to alert the police. Faggus was relaxing over his beer, and Winnie was in the stables enjoying her oats, when four constables burst in and seized him. They thought they had him, but hadn't bargained on Winnie coming to her master's rescue. When Winnie heard his shrill whistle she gave up on her oats, kicked down the door of her stable and burst into the pub. The constables were terrified of the extraordinary mare, and released Faggus who leapt onto Winnie's back and made his escape.

The Long Bridge at Barnstaple is so named because it is a sixteen span structure over the river Taw. Perhaps Faggus's most spectacular escape was one day when he was heading out of Barnstaple towards Sticklepath, and when he and Winnie were on the bridge he realised they were trapped because there were constables sealing it at both ends. At last Faggus was trapped, or so it seemed, until he urged his extraordinary horse forward and she leapt off the bridge and dropped forty feet into the river Taw with a huge splash. Winnie swam to shore and carried her soaked master to safety.

The Long Bridge, Barnstaple over the River Taw

One of the best known stories about Tom Faggus describes how he held up Mr Bampfylde of North Molton who was the man to whom he had lost the legal battle which cost him his fiancee and his living as a blacksmith.

Bampfylde produced his valuables, and handed them to the highwayman who examined them and handed them back to the frightened local notable with the remark, "Permit me the pleasure sir of honouring the custom that a robber never robs a robber".

The Robin Hood style highwayman eventually found himself in a trap he couldn't escape from. A constable disguised as a beggar accepted a drink bought for him by Faggus in a tavern at Exebridge, then kicked his chair from under him. His colleagues rushed in and the outlaw was outnumbered and trapped. He whistled for Winnie, but by now the mare's abilities were well known, and a constable shot her before she could intervene and rescue her master.

There is no confirmed record of it, but it is said that Tom Faggus was tried and hanged in Taunton in 1671.

One of the Westcountry's most colourful rogues, who is never recorded as having used violence as a highwayman, met an end many would consider undeserved, and everyone would agree that Winnie didn't deserve to be shot!

CHAPTER SIX

John Fall

One of the few things attributed to the alleged highwayman John Fall is the name of a crossroads called Beetor Cross in Devon which is also known as the 'Watching Place'! This crossroads is now quiet and peaceful, but it once lay on the main road between Tavistock and Exeter, and is alleged to be where John Fall used to lie hidden and watch, and wait for unwary travellers who became his victims.

'The Watching Place', Beetor Cross, Devon

Another version of how the crossroads came by its name is that there used to be a gallows there where convicted highwaymen and other outlaws were hanged. The friends and relatives of those left hanging as an example to others would watch from in hiding, and then when they were sure they weren't seen, they would cut the body down and remove it for burial.

'The Watching Place Crossroads'

Of all the names of scoundrels in this short book John Fall is in one way the most intriguing, as I only managed to find two single references to him. One on a website listing highwaymen hauntings in the Westcountry, and the other in *Crossings Guide to Dartmoor* which mentions him as follows, "This part of the road was once the haunt of a mysterious individual named John Fall, who seems to have been a highwayman with a penchant for frightening his victims by a kind of Spring-heel Jack performance".

Perhaps the spirit of John Fall, the most enigmatic of the highwaymen, still watches from his 'Watching Place', together with the other ghosts said to haunt the crossroads. There is no record of what happened to John Fall, he may have ended up on the gallows at "the Watching Place" or he may have evaded justice.

CHAPTER SEVEN

John Fitz

Sir John Fitz came into the world in 1570 or 1575, confusingly both dates are mentioned in various places. He was born into a rich aristocratic land owning family which in those days owned much of the town of Tavistock and the land around it. Although he started life with every advantage he developed into a murdering, dissolute, whoring bully who terrorised the town for several years, until in 1605 he spectacularly committed suicide. There is a full statue of John Fitz and his wife Mary with the young John, later Sir John kneeling beside them, in St. Eustacius Church in Tavistock.

John Fitz Senior died in 1590 and and left his entire fortune to his son. The new heir to the family estates eventually married Bridget the sixth daughter of the Earl Devon, Sir William Courtenay of Powderham Castle. Their daughter, Mary, was born in 1596 which was the year John came into his full inheritance, and the couple took over Fitzford House in Tavistock. By this time he had already started to gain a fearsome reputation as a bully and hell raiser. Bridget managed to be a sensible calming presence during these early years, but her influence waned as time went by.

John Fitz and wife Mary with their son (kneeling) in St. Eustacius Church

In June 1599 John committed the first of three murders. He was in a drinking session with his friends including a loyal and close friend called Nicholas Slanning of a nearby village called Bickleigh. John got drunker and drunker and started to boast that he owned the freehold of every bit of land on his estates except that owned by her Majesty the Queen. Slanning politely pointed out that John's claim was incorrect because he occupied a small piece of land which actually belonged to him, and on which he could claim rent if he so chose. This caused John Fitz to counter claim that Slanning was not telling the truth, and he flew into a rage, and drew his dagger and threatened his drinking companion. The others at the table intervened and calmed Fitz down, and eventually the party broke up and Slanning left for Bickleigh with one of his men. Fitz and his friends carried on drinking and Fitz decided that Slanning had insulted him and he wanted revenge. They chased after Slanning, caught him, and egged on by his drinking pals, Fitz killed him with a thrust of his sword.

John Fitz was now aged 24 and he fled to France to avoid prosecution for the murder. However, his wife and mother managed to get him a pardon. He then returned to England at the end of 1599, and immediately went back to his old ways.

James I was crowned in 1603 and showered the English gentry and aristocracy with honours to win their favour. Among the recipients was John Fitz who became Sir John. The newly honoured Sir John seemed emboldened by his knighthood, and his reign of terror in Tavistock continued and involved men being attacked and assaulted, women molested, property destroyed, and caused a frightened wariness in the town as Sir John and his gang of dissolutes and desperados did as they pleased. During this period it is believed that Fitz committed his second murder, and Fitzford House started to resemble a cross between a brothel and a lawless tavern.

Fitz's wife Bridget had by now had enough, and she went home to her own family at Powderham Castle with her daughter. This marked the start of Sir John's past starting to catch up with him. Sir William Courtenay, his father-in-law started investigating him to determine whether he had stolen or improperly used any of his daughter's property. Nicholas Slanning's two sons and his daughter sued Sir John for compensation due to his having killed their father. Even though he now had a title his pardon for killing Slanning had not been fully ratified, and Sir John began to fear for his future. He decided to go to London to seek legal and other advice. He left Tavistock with a footman in attendance and started on the long ride to the east.

As his journey progressed Sir John became more and more apprehensive and the long hours on the road provided plenty of time for him to dwell on his corrupt dissolute life, his murders, and the fate that might await him. He struggled to sleep at night and what sleep he did achieve was occupied by nightmares. The ghost of Slanning haunted him, and he was heard shrieking in anguish as he lay drenched in sweat in his bed.

Nearing London in the early hours one morning he found a small inn called The Anchor at Twickenham. Everyone in the Anchor was asleep but Sir John pounded on the door until the innkeeper, Daniel Alley, opened up for him. Alley tried to protest that all the beds were taken, and the inn was not appropriate accommodation for a man of Sir John's standing in society. Fitz insisted and in the end Daniel Alley gave up his own room, and sent his wife to sleep with the children. Fitz couldn't sleep and he convinced Daniel to stay up and talk during the night. After dawn had broken poor Daniel, who had had virtually no sleep, was outside at the water pump getting ready to go to work when Fitz rushed at him with his sword drawn. Why Fitz saw Alley as a threat is not recorded, but by then Fitz was clearly mentally ill. He killed Daniel Alley with his sword, and then when his wife rushed to her husband's side he stabbed her aswell, although mercifully he only wounded her.

The mists in his clouded mind cleared and he realised what he had done. Sir John Fitz then went to a wall and wedged the hilt of his sword into a crack so that the blade pointed outwards. He took a few steps back and then ran at the blade stabbing himself right through the chest. This did not kill him and he withdrew the sword from his body, once again wedged it into the wall, and tried a second time. He still did not manage to kill himself, and was taken into the inn by neighbours and treated by a doctor. He lived for two more days but eventually his wounds overcame him. Even though he had committed two, maybe three murders and had an evil reputation, due to his rank in society he was interred in the chancel of St. Mary's, Twickenham on Augusty 10th 1605.

CHAPTER EIGHT

The Clovelly Cannibals (The Gregg Family)

The most grisly story in this book is certainly that of the cannibals of Clovelly, the Gregg family. Opinion is divided as to whether the family really existed, and if so whether the tales attributed to them are true. Interestingly the acitivities of John Gregg and his family almost mirror those of another family of alleged murderers and cannibals in Scotland headed by a man called Sawney Beane. One theory is that the Beane story 'inspired' the Gregg one, but some researchers appear to believe that neither is true. A plausible explanation that is often advanced as to why the Gregg story was invented is that the existence of Clovelly's family of murdering cannibals was publicised by local smugglers, robbers and pirates to help keep the area free of visitors and law officers.

A booklet published around 1770 called *The History of John Gregg, and His Family of Robbers and Murderers* seems to be the earliest published account of the Greggs. The booklet claims that John Gregg was born near Exeter, and as a young man he worked in agriculture. However, he was lazy and soon left home taking with him a woman who would turn out to be just as depraved and vicious as he was. They made their home in a large cave on the sea shore near Clovelly. The cave had a narrow entrance which led into a winding passage which eventually reached a large cavern.

Clovelly, Devon

Nature Walk to Clovelly

The Greggs lived in their cave for twenty five years, during which time they produced fourteen children and over thirty grandchildren. The whole family lived by robbery and murder, and their murder victims weren't only people they stole from, they were also a food source, the Greggs were early Hannibal Lecters, they ate their victims! The inhabitants of the area lived in fear of the Greggs, and the population thinned out because people kept disappearing and others decided there were safer places to live and left.

The 1770 booklet claimed that in their twenty five year reign of terror the Greggs killed around a thousand victims. Their end came when one evening they attacked a husband and wife returning home on horseback on the road. They dragged the wife off the horse and killed her, but the husband fought hard and was rescued when, by lucky chance, a large group of travellers appeared. The travellers outnumbered the Greggs who ran away, but the incident triggered an approach by locals to the Mayor of Exeter to ask for his help in bringing the Greggs to justice. The mayor sent word to the King, and the King sent four hundred soldiers to Clovelly. Eventually after several days searching, bloodhounds working with the soldiers discovered the entrance to the Gregg's cave. A subterranean hell was revealed when the soldiers went inside the cavern. Bones and bits of bodies were widely scattered, and in places bodies were hung like animal carcasses in butcher shops.

The entire Gregg clan was present in the cave, and they were all arrested and taken to Exeter. Some accounts say the whole family was hanged, and others that they were burnt in groups. Although there are accounts of the mass hanging of the Greggs, there doesn't appear to be official records of this nor, apparently, are there records of a large force of soldiers being dispatched by the king, or of the king's attendance which is mentioned in one account.

The story of the Clovelly Cannibals seems farfetched even for folklore, but curiously a stretch of Clovelly Bay is known as "the Devil's Kitchen". That the local Clovelly crooks heard the sory of Sawney Beane, and adapted it for their own use to keep prying eyes away from witnessing their smuggling, robbery, and other illegal activities seems the most likely explanation.

CHAPTER NINE

The Gubbins of Dartmoor

The Gubbins were said to be a notorious band of cutthroats, footpads, sheep rustlers and thieves who lived as an independent community in the Lydford Gorge/Brentor region of Dartmoor. They moved into the area during the fifteenth century, and consolidated their influence and hold on the region in the sixteenth century. At one time the leader of the Gubbins had the nickname, the king of the Gubbins. The names Gubbins, Gubbings, Gybbins, and Gubbinses were all used when referring to what became known as a tribe of savages. According to folklore the Gubbins community may have started earlier in the 1300's when two pregnant prostitues ran away to the moor. They were joined by "lewd menfolk", and without constraints of church or marriages the numbers increased and the tribe was born. At one time the Gubbins were commanded by Roger Rowle, but legend and folklore do not make clear whether Rowle was not only the commander of the Gubbins, but was also the 'king' of the band.

As with much legend and folklore it is very difficult to separate fact from fiction. However, from all accounts a broadbrush summary of the Gubbins would be that this fierce, hovel, hut, and cave dwelling community may have started on Dartmoor in the 1300's, increased their numbers and consolidated their power in the 1400's (15th Century), ruled a large, almost independent, area of Devon in the 1500's (16th Century), and then started to die out and largely disappear after the English Civil War (1642-1651). It is said that by the beginning of Charles 1st reign their numbers had grown to many hundreds, and they effectively ruled over a large part of Dartmoor and its surrounding area. It appears that the Gubbins were almost running a mini country within a country!

Roger Rowle and the Gubbins were fiercely loyal to Charles 1st, and from time to time fought on the royalist side in the Civil War. Rowle's Pool near the Devil's Cauldron in Lydford Gorge bears his name, and is at least some proof that he and his clan existed. Rowle appears to have been something of a Devonian Robin Hood, and although he was a thoroughly lawless character he, reputedly, helped the poorest living in his area of influence.

Charles Kingsley's *Westward Ho*, William Brown's poem *Lydford Journey*, and Anna Eliza Bray's novel *Warleigh*(1830) all refer to the Gubbins. Anna Bray treats the Gubbins very kindly, and in her novel explains how the Gubbins went from being worthy local squires to becoming outlaws. Bray writes of the seduction of John Gubbins' daughter by an officer in King Charles' army and of her betrayal. The Gubbins complained to Sir Richard Grenville, the local commander, and instead of punishing his officer, Grenville arrested and jailed several Gubbins men. Roger Rowle attacked the prison and got the Gubbins out, and this triggered a relentless pursuit by Grenville who eventually caught John Gubbins and hanged him. This in turn sent Rowle on the revenge trail, and he started by killing the officer who had seduced the Gubbins girl.

Thomas Fuller's book *History of the Worthies of England* was published in 1662, and he was considerably less kind to the Gubbins that Bray would later be in her novel. In Fuller's day a common meaning of the word 'gubbings' was scraps of fish of little value. Fuller thought that the family had been named Gubbins to equate them with being of low worth or value.

Anna Bray lived in Tavistock for twenty five years, and clearly did a considerable amount of research to support her novel. Towards the end of her book she wrote "The writer of these pages has been assured that within the last century several of their descendents (who still bore their uncouth name) lived near Brentor, and retained the rude and even savage character of their ancestors".

Whitelady Falls at Lydford Gorge

Indeed records show that in the eighteenth century there were people called Gubbins living in the Lydford area. In 1745 and 1761 the names George Gubbins and Mary Gubbins appeared as witnesses on local legal documents. There is therefore evidence that the Gubbins existed, and there is no reason not to believe that they were a large family which lived semi-wild on Dartmoor for a long time existing on poaching, sheep stealing,preying on travellers, and many other forms of crime. It is a pity that more is not known about Roger Rowle to back up his image of supporting the poorest and most needy, because then Devon could justifiably stake claim to its own Robin Hood.

The decline and demise of a large Gubbins clan has been attributed to being on the wrong side at the end of the Civil war, improved law enforcement during Cromwell's time, and inbreeding, and most likely to a combination of all three.

CHAPTER TEN

The Gentleman Smuggler

For many reasons Isaac Gulliver stands alone among those covered in this book. His life is well documented, he became a very rich smuggler, businessman, and landowner, he stayed a free man, and apparently was gentle and never hurt anyone.

Isaac Gulliver was born near Trowbridge in Wiltshire in September 1745. During his late teens he spent time at sea including a one year trip to Newfoundland with the fishing fleet from Poole in Dorset. At the age of twenty three he married the daughter of the owner of the Blacksmith's Arms on the Salisbury to Blandford road. It did not take him long to take control of the pub and change its name to the King's Arms. In addition to being a landlord by now Gulliver was developing what would become a lucrative smuggling business. Eventually his smuggling activities would involve fifteen luggers (small coastal ships), and would stretch all along the south coast of England from Poole in the east to Torbay in Devon in the west. Gin, other spirits, lace, silk and tea were all smuggled to various points on England's south coast and distributed using a well organised network.

At the height of his smuggling career Gulliver employed over fifty men to whom he gave special clothing which was almost a uniform. They wore smocks, grew their hair long, tied it in a pony tail, and coloured it white with powder. To employ a large number of men in illegal activities, and dress them all in a kind of livery uniform indicates that Gulliver was more than a little confident he wasn't going to be caught by the Customs men. However, he did have some close shaves with the law. On one occasion it is alleged that when he knew the Customs men were coming to arrest him he lay in an open coffin after having covered his face in white powder. His wife let the Customs men in, showed them her husband's body, and said he had died during the night. The arresting officers left, and Gulliver got out of his coffin and escaped. Later his wife had a mock funeral and buried a coffin filled with stones. Perhaps Isaac was watching his own funeral and laughing his head off?!

Gulliver's houses contained secret concealed rooms for hiding contraband awaiting sale and distribution. Although his activities stretched from Hampshire to Devon, the Bournemouth area was his centre of operations. His men created new paths going inland some of which eventually became part of the road network in the Bournemouth area.

In May 1782 the government offered pardons to smugglers who were either willing to serve in the Royal Navy themselves, or who could provide two substitutes prepared to do so. Gulliver had no trouble putting forward substitutes, but although he had been pardoned he carried on his smuggling operations. One has to wonder why a large easily recognisable well-known man employing several, almost uniformed, smuggling assistants was able to move around openly in complete freedom both before and after his pardon. His men were identifiable and distinctive, and they also appeared to be able to operate with impunity. This could be explained because Customs men were few in numbers but had large areas to cover, and their low wages made them susceptible to being bribed. However, it is also probable that the King may have had a hand in enabling Gulliver to smuggle as openly as he did. It is said that on a trip to France Isaac learned of a plot to assassinate George III. He reported this to the King who had the claim investigated and found it to be true. The plotters were exposed, and in his gratitude the King is alleged to have declared "Let Gulliver smuggle as much as he likes".

In 1788 an official report from the Customs House in Poole to His Majesty's Commissioners of Customs in London said the following. "Gulliver was considered one of the greatest and most notorious smugglers in the west of England and particularly in the spirits and tea trades, but in the year 1782 he took the benefit of his Majesty's proclamation for pardoning such offences, and we are informed dropped that branch of smuggling and afterwards confined himself chiefly to the wine trade which he carried on to a considerable extent having vaults at various places along the coast and in remote inland places".

Isaac Gulliver retired from smuggling just before his sixtieth birthday. His final operation was a truly jaw dropping affair. His three largest luggers dropped anchor off the Bournemouth coast heavily laden with huge quantities of brandy, silk, wine, gin and various luxury goods. The cargo was loaded onto several wagons, and with Gulliver riding at its head the convoy, which was said to have stretched for two miles, made its way inland.

Isaac Gulliver died in September 1822 aged seventy seven. He died a very wealthy man, and left a huge fortune which in today's terms would amount to tens of millions of pounds. His descendants were rich and successful pillars of society, and included a Lt. Governor of Burma, and his daughters married leading bankers. It is perhaps something of an irony that the wealth of a smuggler helped establish such a successful and respectable family.

CHAPTER ELEVEN

Tom King

The Stag Inn in Rackenford near Tiverton in Devon is rumoured to be the oldest pub in Devon and dates back to the 12th century. The Stag's other possible claim to fame is that it was a haunt of Tom King the famous highwayman who was an associate of Dirk Turpin. The website *Helpful Holidays, Devon Highwaymen Hauntings* tells of "the regular visits of a weathy young stranger who spent lavishly at the Stag Inn on food, drink, and entertainment. Much later, villagers discovered they'd hosted the Westcountry highwayman who was tempted away by Dirk Turpin to rob wealthy merchants around London". Probably due to his association with Dick Turpin there are various mentions of King's highway robbery exploits, but this is the only one I have found with a connection to Devon.

It seems that Tom King was born in 1712 and died in 1737 at the very young age of only twenty five. His real name is thought to have been Matthew King, and whether 'Tom' was an alias, a nickname, or stuck having been wrongly recorded, is not known. In some accounts King is also referred to as the "Gentleman" Highwayman and as Captain Tom King. Dick Turpin is probably Britain's best known highwayman and it is being linked to Turpin that accounts for much of King's notoriety. One version of the story is that Dick Turpin mistook King for a wealthy potential victim and tried to rob him, and instead they became partners in crime. Apparently until he met King, Dick

Turpin was a relatively low level petty criminal, and it was King who "upgraded" Turpin into being a real highwayman. The pair operated mainly in and around London and in Essex, and their first joint venture crime was alleged to be the theft of a race horse called White Stockings. According to legend the pair had a base in a cave in Epping Forest in Essex which served as their main hideout.

In early May 1737 during a robbery that went wrong, Tom King was shot and wounded in the shoulder, some accounts say that it was Dick Turpin who shot his partner in crime by mistake. King's wound was treated at New Prison in Clerkenwell, but he died on May 19th, and was buried at St. James churchyard in Clerkenwell on May 21st 1737. Tom King left everything he had to his wife Elizabeth.

After King's death Dick Turpin fled to the North of England and was executed two years later in 1739 for stealing horses.

It seems that Tom King's connection to Devon and Rackenford is tenuous, but as part of my research I much enjoyed a visit to the Stag Inn!

The Stag Inn at Rackenford, Devon

CHAPTER TWELVE

John "Babbacombe" Lee (The man they couldn't hang)

A more modern figure than the others in this book is John 'Babbacombe' Lee, the man they couldn't hang! I confess to having included Lee because I found the description "the man they couldn't hang' very intriguing and decided to investigate.

Lee acquired the moniker 'Babbacombe' after he was found guilty of having carried out the Babbacombe murder which occurred on November 15th 1884. It was alleged that he had killed an elderly spinster called Emma Keyse who was his employer. He was sentenced to hang at Exeter on the 23rd of February 1885. He survived three attempts to hang him after which his sentenced was commuted to life. He was eventually released from Portland Prison on December 18th 1907. The reason given for the failure in carrying out Lee's death sentence was "technical". Infact it seems likely that the trap doors, on which stood the man about to die, didn't open and allow the body to drop. One theory often advanced to explain this is that the wooden doors had been soaked and expanded and "welded" themselves together. The Home Office conducted an investigation into why the trap doors failed to open, and they found that the draw bar was out of alignment, and this prevented the hinges opening properly. Basically the evidence on which Lee had been convicted was flimsy. He had been the only man in the house at the time of the killing, he had a previous criminal record for theft, and had a wound on his arm. There must be doubt as to whether Lee was really the killer, and if so it would perhaps have been appropriate that divine intervention prevented the trap doors from opening!

After his release from Portland Prison he became something of a celebrity and used his fame to make a living. He described his having escaped death at the end of a noose as a miracle, and toured the country giving talks and lectures on his life. A short film was made about him, and he wrote a book called *The Man They Couldn't Hang*. Lee was born in Abbotskerwell in Devon in 1864 and died in the United States on March 19th 1945.

Like many of the stories in this book the true story of John Lee is shrouded in mystery. Many regarded his book as being full of fanciful invention. Was he a murderer, and why was the executioner not able to hang him? Whatever the truth it is certain that Lee was not a very nice man. He was suspected of being a thief when in the Royal Navy, and in 1883 he was convicted of theft and sentenced to hard labour. He was then, rightly or wrongly, convicted of murder and soon after his release he married Jessie Bulled. Within a few years he dumped his wife and left her destitute. He then had an affair with another woman who he claimed to be his wife, and they emigrated to America. He was a liar, conman, manipulator, and maybe a murderer. The man they couldn't hang was definitely not a saint, and his deliverance from the hangman was not the "miracle" he claimed!

County Gaol, Exeter. The arrow points to the roof where hangings were carried out.

CHAPTER THIRTEEN

Jack Rattenbury

Unlike many of the characters I have written about in this book, in the case of Jack Rattenbury there is a lot of hard fact. His exploits as a smuggler and privateer are well-recorded and he wrote a book about his life, called *Memoirs of a Smuggler*, which provides more information. He was born in the coastal town of Beer in Devon in 1778 and was baptised in that town on the 18th of October. His father was a shoemaker who left his mother while she was pregnant and went to sea never to return. His mother supported herself and her baby by selling fish and doing odd jobs. Jack first started going to sea on his uncle's fishing boat when he was about nine. He worked as a child apprentice on a couple of fishing vessels at home, before going to Torquay when he was twelve or thirteen to join a privateer called the *Dover* bound for the Azores. In many ways privateers can be described as licensed pirates. These ships were privately owned armed merchant vessels which were given commissions by the sovereign to carry out acts of war at sea. These commissions were known as letters of marque.

Although privateers were operating legally as far as their own governments were concerned, foreign ships would often regard them as hostile and as pirates. After a few months of unsuccessul operations the *Dover* was captured by a better armed French ship, and the vessel and men were taken to Bordeaux where the crew were imprisoned. Young Jack escaped confinement, and about two years later when he was nearly sixteen he made it home to Beer and his mother.

Compared to his two years of adventure, life in Beer was dull, and six months after returning home Jack had started doing a little smuggling at which he was initially quite successful. However, when the opportunity of going back to sea presented itself Jack grabbed it, and signed up on a square rigger that was sailing from Bridport in Dorset to Tenby in Wales to pick up a cargo of anthracite. The vessel was still in the English Channel when once again Jack found himself at odds with the French. His vessel was captured, and the French captain took all the crew off the boat and locked them up aboard his own ship, leaving only Jack and a small boy onboard the English ship together with five Frenchmen. The French crew were ordered to take the English ship to the nearest French port. It soon became apparent that the French didn't know the English coast, and were often close to getting into difficulties. Jack offered to pilot the vessel and his offer was accepted. The French clearly didn't know where they were, and Jack's plan was to take the vessel back to an English port without his captors realising what was going on. There were several occasions when Jack's course and the whereabouts of the ship were questioned by the French, but eventually he managed to steer the ship into Swanage and jump overboard. He made it to shore and alerted the authorities, and a customs cutter sailed after the French and recaptured the ship.

The owner got his vessel back from the authorities by paying salvage, and Jack was thrilled at the part he had played in saving the vessel. He became less thrilled when it became obvious that the owners did not intend to reward his efforts in any way, financially or otherwise.

His next adventure was being pressganged into the Royal Navy, but he soon jumped ship and made his way back to Beer, where for the next five years he made his living fishing and smuggling. In February 1799 he enlisted on a Topsham fishing vessel bound for Newfoundland. Eventually they sailed back across the Atlantic heading for Portugal, where they intended to sell their catch of cod, but they were captured by a Spanish privateer and taken to Vigo. Getting out of difficult situations had become routine for Jack who quickly made friends with his Spanish captors and talked his way into being released.

He got passage on a schooner heading for Guernsey but gales blew them off course and they ended up in southern Ireland before continuing to Guernsey where they arrived three weeks late. He had been away from home this time for a year.

In April 1800 Jack Rattenbury married Anna Partridge, but he couldn't find local employment so he signed on as a privateersman on a lugger which sailed for the Azores the following month. There was no profit from the trip, and for the next several years he made a living smuggling, and sometimes went to sea as a privateer. Jack was operating on the wrong side of the law most of the time, and in July 1806 he appeared before the Falmouth Magistrates Court and received a prison sentence. He escaped and once again made his way back home to Beer.

As he went on through life Jack did not slow down, and escapades and adventures followed one after the other. He made a living as a publican, smuggler, privateer, leisure cruise captain, fisherman, and marine pilot. He served prison terms in Exeter and Dorchester gaols.

Known by some as the Westcountry's Rob Roy, he was the father of at least four children, and remains one of South Devon's most colourful and likeable rogues. In Beer the village commemorated him with Rattenbury Day, and Rattenbury's Cottage which was built in 1820 still stands. The lifelong smuggler and adventurer died aged 65, and is said to have been buried in Seaton church, although other accounts have the nearby Branscombe church as his final resting place.

When Steve and Frances Lee bought the Shepherd's Cottage in Beer in 1988 they didn't realise the house was already occupied – by a ghost. Soon after moving in they started being woken each night in the early hours by loud crashes. Neither Steve nor Frances smoked a pipe, and neither drank whisky but, on a regular basis, they started noticing smells in various places around the house. The present day building had originally been four or five hovels which dated back hundreds of years.

Shepherd's Cottage, Beer, Devon

Steve Lee didn't believe in ghosts but Frances did, and she was not only hearing the early morning crashes, and smelling the whisky and tobacco, she was also feeling a strange and angry presence. She mentioned her haunting suspicions to a neighbour who offered to put her in touch with a local medium called Veronica. Veronica identified the ghost as being a smuggler and a fisherman, and given that the Shepherd's Cottage was locally believed to have been lived in by Jack Rattenbury, it seemed the Lees were sharing their new house with the Rob Roy of the West. The medium persuaded Jack to leave the Lees alone, and Jack said he would, but asked if he could visit from time to time! The crashes stopped but the smells persisted for a while so it seems that Jack kept his word. Jack had admitted to the medium that he was angry that people were in his house and wanted to get rid of the Lees. The other footnote to the story is that the smell of boiling fish was often noticed, and the medium told Frances this was Jack's wife trying to attract their attention!

CHAPTER FOURTEEN

Jack Withrington

Jack Withrington was the youngest of five brothers, and I am not sure if it is accurate to say that it is unique in English history, but all five brothers were hanged as criminals. Jack Withrington started his working life in the leather trade working as a 'tanner', which involved turning animal hides into workable leather.

He became a soldier during Monmouth's rebellion and did well in his regiment. He moved to London and fought duels which established his reputation as a fearless fighting man. However he overstepped the mark when he challenged his captain to a duel and got thrown out of his regiment. Withrington turned to gambling as a means of making a living and initially he was successful. However when his luck or skill sometimes deserted him he took to cheating, and soon no one would play cards with him.

This led to a career change when he decided to try his luck as a highwayman. He invested in a horse, weapons, and other equipment and went looking for his first victim.

He waylaid a farmer and took £40.00 from him which in those days was a very large sum of money, and the fact that the farmer was carrying a large sum may have indicated that he was on his way to or from market. Withrington's next adventure occurred on the Devonshire road beween Chudleigh and Ashburton. The man he held up was Mr Edward Clark who was the usher to the Duchess of Mazarin. He took eight guineas from Clark who offered resistance, and in the scuffle Withrington's mask fell off and Clark recognised him, so the evidence against the highwayman had started being gathered. Within a short time Jack Withrington had become one of England's most notorious highway robbers, but his career behind the mask came to an end when he fell in love with a widow in Bristol who was the innkeeper of the Swan Public House. Unfortunately his life as a publican ended when he was recognised for what he had been, and the lady innkeeper was informed she was living with a once infamous highwayman who she immediately threw out.

Jack reverted to his old pastime, and went back to being an armed highway robber. He ranged far and wide, and waylaid travellers in the Westcountry, and from Hertfordshire to Hounslow. His last robbery occurred on Hounslow Heath when he stopped a nobleman and his two footmen and stole two hundred and eight guineas, sixty pounds in silver, and a package of fine linen. This robbery produced a widespread reaction, and determined pursuit. Jack was caught and arrested at Malmesbury in Wiltshire, and then he was moved to London to face trial. He was found guilty, condemned to death and executed at Tyburn on April 1st 1691.

Jack and his four brothers were all born at Blandford in Dorset, and all four of the brothers were hanged in the county. Jack was the only one to have the distinction of being hanged in the nation's capital, and of having his execution officially recorded in the Newgate Calendar.

The Highwayman's Haunt near Newton Abbot claims to have been a favourite resting place for Jack Withrington, and tradition has it that the highwayman referred to in the pub name is Jack himself.

The Highwayman's Haunt Pub nr Newton Abbott (old photo)

Dick Turpin and his mare, Black Bess

Tom King

John 'Babbacombe' Lee – The Man They Couldn't Hang

Isaac Gulliver – The Gentleman Smuggler

Old Map of Devon & Cornwall
1600/1700's

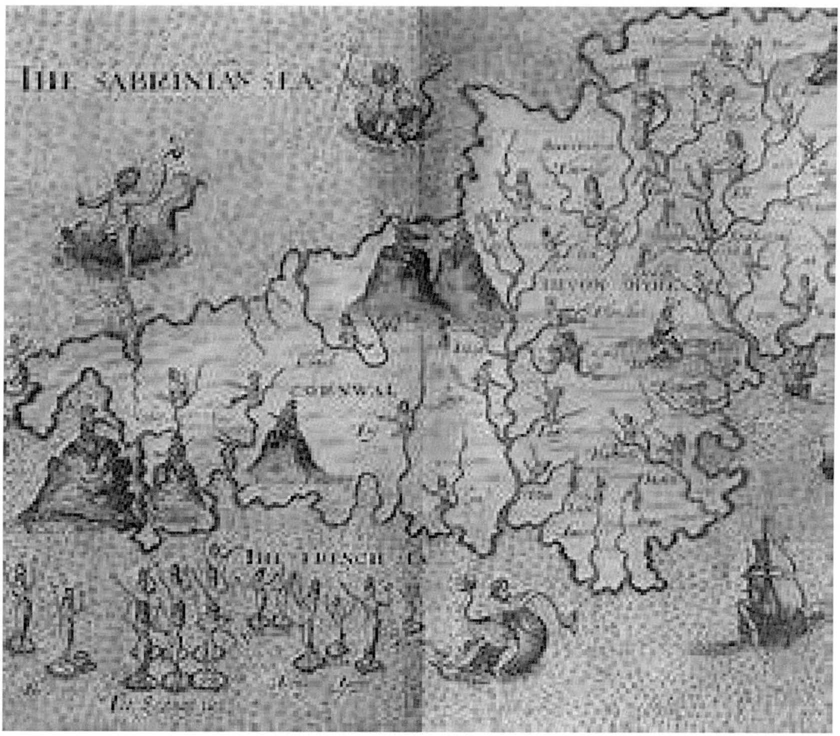

"Stand and Deliver"